generosity
➔ moving toward life that is truly life

a four-week devotional by
Gordon MacDonald
with Patrick Johnson of The National Christian Foundation

Authors: Gordon MacDonald, with Patrick Johnson of The National
Christian Foundation

Published by The National Christian Foundation
11625 Rainwater Drive, Suite 500
Alpharetta, GA 30009
800.681.6223
www.nationalchristian.com

To order copies for your church,
visit GenerousChurch.com

Command those who are rich
in this present world not to be arrogant
nor to put their hope in wealth,
which is so uncertain, but to put their
hope in God, who richly provides us
with everything for our enjoyment.

Command them to do good, to be
rich in good deeds, and to be generous
and willing to share. In this way they
will lay up treasure for themselves as
a firm foundation for the coming age,
so that they may take hold of the
life that is truly life.

1 Timothy 6:17-19

contents

moving toward
generosity
an introduction by Patrick Johnson of The National Christian Foundation

Generosity...what a simple, splendid word. And how special it is to know that generosity is a gift to us from the first and ultimate giver, God. From the very beginning, He has unfolded His sovereign plan of creation, love, grace, and salvation as an expression of His abundant generosity, and He invites each one of us to participate in this with Him as He continues to move through history.

Inside the soul of every Christian is a God-inspired desire for the generous life, for a life tailored around His example of selflessness and sacrifice. We are all on a spiritual journey, and we are all on a giving journey. Both are filled with growth and movement. We encounter times of expansion. We transition away from the old to the new. We move forward in our generosity, learning to give more and give more sacrificially.

But as with any journey, we get caught in periods of stagnation and decline. The pull of culture and our own flesh often conspire against us to stifle our attempts at living truly generous lives. We need the power of God's Word, His Spirit, and fellow believers to emerge into a new time of flourishing progression.

God started my family on our giving journey almost six years ago. And quite frankly, it hasn't been easy. There have been highs and lows, periods of surplus and scarcity, times when I've been obedient and times when I've failed. Yet God, rich in His amazing grace, has never let me down or let me go. I still push on, moving forward, moving toward true life...the joyful, generous life I believe He is calling me to live.

The act of moving often signifies a passageway to something better. This is certainly what has happened in my family, and this is what I want for you over the next 30 days – to recognize God's wonderful gift of generosity and how it can transform us and those we influence to become more like Him. Paul described this generous life in I Timothy 6:19 as the "life that is truly life."

the act of moving often signifies a passageway to something better

So where do we start?
...with an excellent teacher. For years, I've admired Gordon MacDonald's ability to take God's Word and draw out rich truths of generosity. I knew Gordon's writings in this book would help all of us move forward in our quest for the true, generous life.

So how do we move?
...day by day, week by week. This book is broken down into four weeklong segments, each containing seven daily devotions. Because generosity is normally best accomplished in the context of community, I encourage you spend the next month reflecting on these devotions with a family member, friend, small group, or church class. Together, you'll also read twelve "forward thinking" key principles and four incredibly inspirational stories of people that moved toward life that is truly life in powerful ways.

Ok, enough introduction. *Let's move.*

moving toward
transformation

moving toward
transformation

God made the first move of generosity.

And the second. And the third.

From the moment He imparted life to mankind to the climactic gift of salvation through the death of His Son Jesus Christ, God has set the supreme example of radical, sacrificial giving for His followers.

The word sacrifice is so difficult for us to accept, at times. Yet that's exactly what we must do when we practice generosity: sacrifice something of value to us for the good of another, because we love them. You see, this is what differentiates generosity and giving. Giving can be done begrudgingly and devoid of love. But true generosity is always initiated by love. Because God is love, as our hearts become molded in His likeness, we will naturally move toward a life of greater generosity.

Over the next seven days, we will explore the incredible generosity of the Trinity – Father, Son, and Holy Spirit. We'll see in Scripture that just as God is love, God is generous. In fact, His extravagant generosity flows out of His extravagant love. God the Father is the first generous giver, God the Son is the chief of generous givers, and God the Holy Spirit is the ongoing expression of God's generosity in us.

We will also explore how the early church – comprised of regular people like you and me – was absolutely transformed by the grace of God for lives of radical generosity. Barnabas (Acts 4:36-37) and Mary of Bethany (John 12:3) are two examples of early Christians who viewed their wealth through the eyes of eternity and were determined to live generous lives because of it.

So before we move forward in the act of generous giving, we must move forward in the transformation of our hearts, souls, and minds...a transformation by the truth that God made the first generous move.

forward thinking — God is the first and most generous giver.

God, the first and most generous

"For God so loved the world that He gave His one and only Son,
that whoever believes in Him shall not perish but have eternal life."

John 3:16

This verse follows on the heels of a conversation between Jesus and Nicodemus, a Jewish leader. It was a conversation that happened in the nighttime hours because Nicodemus was not yet prepared to risk his reputation by being seen with the Lord in public.

For God so loved the world. Are these words and what follows an extension of the Nicodemus conversation or a comment that flows from it? We do not know. But what is universally accepted is that we are reading some of the most profound of all Biblical truths. God loved...God gave His Son...Whoever believes possesses eternal life. We call it the Gospel. It's that simple! It's that profound.

If we wish to become generous givers, then we must know this Scripture intimately. It reminds us that God does not ask of us anything that He has not first done for us. God is the first generous giver. He has provided the highest model of generosity, and He calls for Biblical people to follow.

forward thinking

We are most like God
when we give.

The generous giver is someone whose heart generates love. It is not a sentimental or romantic love, but a love built on compassion and care, a love that is drawn to the broken and fragmented creatures and conditions of our world. This kind of love values human beings as those created in God's image. It is accompanied by a righteous anger at systems and forces that perpetuate the suffering and ignorance of others. This kind of love cannot contain itself when there are opportunities to change lives and circumstances for those unable to change their own situation.

Following God's example, the generous giver gives out of his or her very best. God gave His only Son; we give from the depths of our resources and abilities. We give not a token of our wealth, but sacrificially. As God sacrificed His Son, so we follow and give even those things that are most precious to us in our personal worlds: our time, our convenience, our creature comforts.

Finally, the generous giver is someone who, in a sense, lays the tracks for others to find eternal life. We do not give eternal life (only God does this), but we give that which makes it possible for others to find eternal life. As Biblical people we believe that a solid proportion of our giving should move in the direction of those activities that make Christ known, and help others to know what it means to follow.

It is the will of God that we become generous givers. But He would never ask us to do what He has not first done for us.

What are two ways God has been extravagantly generous to you? What impact have these gifts had on your life?

Jesus, the chief of generous givers

I am not commanding you, but I want to test the sincerity of your love by
comparing it with the earnestness of others. For you know the grace of our
Lord Jesus Christ, that though He was rich, yet for your sakes He became poor,
so that you through His poverty might become rich.

2 Corinthians 8:8-9

Imagine sitting in the congregation when Paul's letter to the Corinthian people was first read. Are the Corinthian Christians squirming as he pokes and prods at their spiritual resilience? They were a boastful, self-confident people. They reveled in their size, their accumulative talents, the sophistication of their people.

"I want to test the sincerity of your love," Paul wrote. And how does he do it? By making some comparisons. To the Macedonians, in fact; and apparently, they failed the test.

But then Paul made an even more challenging comparison. "You know the grace of our Lord Jesus Christ," he wrote. Presumably they did, but Paul described it anyway: He who was rich chose to become poor so that you might become spiritually rich. There is here what some might call a transfer of wealth – from heaven to Corinth. Jesus was the chief of generous givers.

The Bible is not easy on us when it comes to this business of generosity. We are instinctively selfish people. At first God set the bar low when it came to mandatory giving: a tithe, ten percent of one's holdings. However, generous giving is another story. Generous giving starts when it hurts to give. When one moves in the direction of "poverty" in order to make someone else "rich."

By richness we are not talking about adding to someone else's net worth. Rather we are talking about spiritual richness or the richness that comes from living the life that God intended for all (not just the privileged) to live. Jesus set the pace in His incarnation and His atonement at the cross. He went from wealth to poverty that we might go from poverty to wealth. That is our model. That is our call.

Think of Christ; think of grace. He came to the world as a "rich" person. As Son of God, He was rich in position; as heir of all the treasures of heaven, Jesus was rich in inheritance. Prior to His incarnation, there is nothing He did not know, nothing He could not do; no one possessed greater amounts of power and knowledge. However, He exchanged all this richness for a form of poverty. "He became poor." Poor, how? He became the sacrificial Lamb of God and forfeited His life that out of the atoning work of the cross, spiritually poor people (each of us) might become rich.

Genuine Christianity compels the true Christian to become a generous person because the central act of our faith is an act of generosity. "He became poor that we might become rich." It cost Christ to transfer wealth-of-spirit to us.

The generous giver knows and understands that giving does not begin until there is sacrifice in alignment with the sacrifice of Christ. The Corinthians apparently never figured this out; the Thessalonians did. Perhaps it explains why one church was always sickly (the bigger and the wealthier church) and the other seems to have had a vigorous and exemplary life.

Describe an example from your life when you have given generously. What impact did this have on both you and the recipient?

Jesus, ultimate downward mobility

Your attitude should be the same as that of Christ Jesus: Who, being in very
nature God, did not consider equality with God something to be grasped,
but made Himself nothing, taking the very nature of a servant, being made
in human likeness and being found in appearance as a man, He humbled
Himself and became obedient to death – even death on a cross!

Philippians 2:5-8

When a commander gave his charge to his troops just before battle,
it was not unusual for him to cite the exploits of a past hero. He
would remind his people of a brave soldier who had given everything – perhaps his own life – in order to win the battle. Nothing
motivated men better than the model of a great soldier.

Perhaps this is why Paul turned his attention to Jesus. Asking
the Philippians to climb a notch higher in their life together, Paul
appealed to the greatest of all generous givers: Jesus himself.

Here is the perfect picture of the generous giving sequence. Jesus,
being in the very nature of God, is the consummate picture of
wealth as the Prince of heaven. But He did not hold on to what
was rightfully His; He relinquished it. Then, having surrendered
His privileges, He actually descended from His privileged position
in the godhead to become not just a man but a slave. And died not
the death of a normal slave but that of a criminal, sacrificed on the
cross. From the highest of the high to the lowest of the low. Some
have called this ultimate downward mobility.

Who of us could ever attain to this? Yet here we have the perfect
picture to what the generous giver is called to – a life of giving that
has Christ as its model. But that is not the end. For Paul shifted the
picture back to the Heavenly Father. Therefore, God exalted Him
(back) to the highest place. This is the resurrection and the exal-
tation due to Jesus when He ascended into heaven. There He has

been given the name above every name. And this one who became a slave and a sacrifice becomes the one before whom all nations bow. He is the one who is ultimately designated Lord of all.

From the highest to the lowest and back to the highest. It is the great hymn of the generous giver. It is the reminder of what great sacrifice there is in generous giving. And it is the promise that the generous giver is never lost from the sight of God. That which is given away is but a small pittance compared to that which will be fully gained when we stand before God and hear Him say to His troops, "well done!"

What are some examples of how Jesus modeled generosity to His followers?

Jesus, God of basin and towel

Jesus knew that the Father had put all things under His power, and that
He had come from God and was returning to God; so He got up from the meal,
took off His outer clothing, and wrapped a towel around His waist. After that,
He poured water into a basin and began to wash His disciples' feet,
drying them with the towel that was wrapped around Him.

John 13:3-5

We come to the final hours of the so-called Holy Week. Before the night was over, Jesus would be – as He had warned – in the hands of angry men who did not rest until He had died.

And yet, there we find Jesus, in a borrowed room where He could spend His final hours with His friends and disciples. Judas – just hours from committing his heinous act – was there. So were the rest of the twelve. None of them was in touch with the importance of the hour. Only the Lord "knew that the time to leave this world" had come.

It was in these moments of the Passover meal that we read, "(Jesus) now showed them the full extent of His love." In a sense Jesus had been showing His love in escalating ways throughout the previous three years. His love had been demonstrated when He picked these men out of the rawness of their lives. He had seen in them qualities that no one else would have seen. He had stayed with them through their failures and betrayals. He had shown patience when they cowered in fear, embarrassed themselves in their selfishness, and reverted to the worst of human nature in arguing about who was the brightest and best. Love is the only word that describes the inclination that the Savior had toward this unruly group. And tonight, here in this upper room, they had shown few signs that everything they learned had yet reached their hearts.

He washed their feet!

The Son of God (read these words slowly and carefully) stripped Himself of His clothes, took the basin and the towel, and set Himself to washing.

Aspiring generous giver, take note. What qualifies as an act as truly generous has relatively little to do with the amount of money one gives. Generous giving begins with the posture of total humility. Here we find the Incarnate Prince of Heaven, of whom the angels sing, who sits at the right hand of Almighty God as Lord of all Creation: on His knees before ordinary men, washing the dirt and grime of Jerusalem's pathways off their dust-encrusted feet. This picture must be riveted into our hearts. It shows us what we must become.

Who is the most generous person you've ever known? What impact has he or she had on your life?

The Holy Spirit, the outpouring of God's love into our hearts

And hope does not disappoint us, because God has poured out
His love into our hearts by the Holy Spirit, whom He has given us.

Romans 5:5

From time to time in the Scriptures, we are reminded that generous giving began in the heart of God. It is at the very core of the effort God made to redeem mankind through the work of Jesus at the cross.

"God has poured out His love into our hearts," Paul wrote. We cannot afford to consign these words to mere theological rhetoric. Paul had experienced this love. Having been raised and trained in a law-conscious frame of thought, he knew what it was like to feel as though he could never measure up. He knew the debilitating demands of a religion that said that one was never good enough.

And then he had come into touch with the grace of the God of Jesus Christ. This was a dimension of Israel's God he'd never known. And once he became aware, he never stopped extolling the praises of a God who led with His love, His generous love. And that is what most of this chapter is about.

This was not a conditional generosity that flowed from heaven. "When we were still powerless," Paul wrote, "Christ died for the ungodly." These familiar words threaten to pass over our heads without the contemplation they deserve. They offer at least two messages to us. The first is that we were and are loved by God, through Christ, even though we have done nothing to deserve His affection. In fact, we have often thwarted that love, much as a teenager who irrationally rebels against his family.

The second thought is equally important: The God who gives to us so generously has provided a pattern of giving for us to adopt. At the heart of our giving is a certain mindset: We are to give to the one in need, the one who is weak, the one who is oppressed not because they beg us to do so...and not because they promise to praise us or flood us with appreciation...and not because we expect immediate results. But we give because we love!

What happens to our gift once given is between the receiver and God. It was ours to give, and our expectations and conditions stop there. If there is return, appreciation, or some remarkable result, so be it. We are permitted to delight in such a moment. But this is not why we give.

We give because God gave. We give as God gave. And we give as generously as God gave. And that requires great maturity and obedience on our part.

What does your current giving reflect about your understanding of God's grace (unmerited favor) in your life?

The early church: a culture of generosity

All the believers were one in heart and mind. No one claimed that any of
His possessions was his own, but they shared everything they had.... There were
no needy persons among them. For from time to time those who owned lands or
houses sold them, brought the money from the sales and put it at the apostles'
feet, and it was distributed to anyone as he had need.

Acts 4:32-35

Luke, author of Acts, traces the growth and development of the first
church, stopping occasionally to give us a paragraph of commentary or overview of how things are going. This is one of the places.
It is a general description of the culture of the followers of Christ
who lived in Jerusalem.

Once again, liberality of spirit dominates the description. And there
may be a reason for this. Luke is writing to a specific audience that
knows little if anything about giving. It is a world that is dominated
by an unfeeling, self-centered perspective toward the poor and
the needy. If one has been shaped by such a world, then these
characterizations of the early Christian community are astonishing.

Centuries before, Plato had advocated a community that might live
with everything held in common. But it had never really happened.

forward thinking

When we give,
the world takes notice.

It was just an idea. But now it was happening! There were people who were actually so committed to one another that they had embraced each other as family.

It is a remarkable thing to be able to say, "there were no needy persons among them." It was this mind and heart perspective that would explain much of the success of the early church. In a heartless world, the generosity and service of the first Christian generations was such a stunning contrast that people everywhere sat up and took notice. It is fair to speculate that Christian generosity and service did more to win people to the Gospel of Christ than all the preaching that was done.

We are told that people liquidated possessions, brought the proceeds to the apostles, and it was distributed to anyone who had need. And as if we needed to personalize this outflow of Christian love, Luke focuses attention on one man, Joseph – soon to be known as Barnabas. He epitomizes what is going on. Selling a field, he brought the entire amount to the apostles with the apparent charge that they should use it for anyone who was struggling.

Generous giving is the foundation of the Christian movement. It was there from the very beginning. Not that well organized – as we shall soon see – it nevertheless was the overflow out of hearts that had found the mercy of Christ. And as they had received mercy, so they felt compelled to give it in practical ways. And Barnabas is the first performer. Watch him! He is what God wishes every man and woman to be.

Read the Malawi story (next page) and answer: What are some tangible ways that today's Christian church can model the generosity of the early Christian church?

the Malawi attraction
one community's journey of sacrificial giving

Generosity is incredibly attractive. Whittier Area Community Church in Southern California experienced this truth recently. Its leaders had a collective vision to build a hospital for orphans in Malawi, a densely populated country in South-Central Africa.

The church's leaders were convinced that God was calling them to collect a special Christmas offering to build the hospital. Yet when they determined that to build such a structure would cost $160,000, they became discouraged because the church's largest-ever Christmas offering in their 35-year history was just $25,000.

Yet they pressed on.

The leaders cast the vision to the congregation, and the whole church got involved in amazing ways. Children set up Malawi lemonade stands in their neighborhoods to raise money. One couple gave the money they previously had set aside for infertility treatments to provide for African children, instead. One woman gave up a full month of physical therapy to join in the contagious spirit of generosity that swept over the church. And on and on. The stories were countless.

Yet, it wasn't just the church members that got engaged. Believers in other congregations and even non-Christians from around the community learned about the Malawi hospital plan. New conversations sparked to life, and soon, giving commitments and words of support began pouring in from everywhere.

At last, the Christmas offering day came. Instead of $25,000 or even $160,000, on that one day Whittier raised over $500,000!

There was such an outpouring of generosity from both within and outside the church that its senior pastor, Bill Ankerberg, later exclaimed joyfully, "Generosity is the new evangelism!"

Indeed it is. But at the same time, this contagious spirit of unbridled generosity has historic roots, most notably in the book of Acts. And like the early Christian church, this modern day church attracted the attention of the world through its abounding pattern of giving.

The Christmas offering day came and the church responded...instead of $25,000 or even $160,000, on that one day the church raised over $500,000!

This causes one to think: How effective would our churches be today at winning the world for Christ if we all displayed the same generosity as the early church...as Whittier Area Community Church?

>>> **Watch a video version of this story at GenerousChurch.com/generosity**

21

Mary – the fragrance of giving

Then Mary took about a pint of pure nard, an expensive perfume;
she poured it on Jesus' feet and wiped His feet with her hair.
And the house was filled with the fragrance of the perfume.

John 12:3

This account in the life of Jesus takes place during what is tradition-ally called Holy Week. Only a few days separate what is described here from the arrest and trial and crucifixion of our Lord.

A dinner was being held "in Jesus' honor," at the house of Lazarus in Bethany, and it is noted, "Martha served." Once an activist, always an activist.

But Mary was there as well, once again at the feet of Jesus. This time the emphasis was not upon listening but worshipping. And her worship was expressed in an act: the pouring of a pint of expensive perfume on the feet of the Lord.

The western and modern mind must bend to fit this story in order to appreciate what was being said here.

The washing of another's feet was an act of ultimate reverence. It was more than a practical act of cleaning the dirt off of dusty feet. It was a signal of worship and adoration. And to do it not with water but with expensive perfume, and to use her hair rather than a towel, compounds the honor to a level we can hardly imagine.

Mary was a consummate generous giver. First, the value of her gift was truly sacrificial. For most women, this perfume was considered something of an insurance policy, something of value stashed away to live on when everything else was gone. If it was not used in this fashion, it was to be employed as a burial perfume, an honorable anointing of the dead.

The value of Mary's gift revealed a level of unbridled devotion. Mary offered not only her treasure to the Lord, but also her public commitment. Her actions made it clear that Jesus was her Lord, and that by her actions she wanted everyone to know her life was in His hands.

Lastly, Mary's gift was an unmistakable witness. The odor of the spent perfume filled the house. No one could be unaware of what she had done, and in Whom she believed.

In a world (both then and now) that often obsesses over techniques and ideologies, Mary is a refreshing woman. She did what others only talk about: she walked her talk. Her love for the Lord had no limits. What she had, what she was, what she could do: Everything was given to Jesus.

How is giving an act of worship and devotion to God in your life?

week 1 discussion

The following is a summary of the ideas and questions from this week's devotions. Use them for personal reflection or small group discussion, and consider journaling to record your thoughts and impressions.

forward thinking

Which of these "forward thinking" points has the most meaning for you? Least meaning? Why?

God is the first and most generous giver.

We are most like God when we give.

When we give, the world takes notice.

impact from the Malawi story

What was the most important thing you learned from the Malawi story? Have you personally experienced the attraction of generous giving? What do you believe God's role is today in shaping the generosity of His children?

reflection questions

1   What are two ways God has been extravagantly generous to you? What impact have these gifts had on your life?

2   Describe an example from your life when you have given generously. What impact did this have on both you and the recipient?

3   What are some examples of how Jesus modeled generosity to His followers?

4   Who is the most generous person you've ever known? What impact has he or she had on your life?

5   What does your current giving reflect about your understanding of God's grace (unmerited favor) in your life?

6   What are some tangible ways that today's Christian church can model the generosity of the early Christian church?

7   How is giving an act of worship and devotion to God in your life?

moving toward

freedom

moving toward

freedom

"For the love of money is a root of all kinds of evil" (1 Timothy 6:10).

In light of this verse, doesn't it stand to reason that the love of *giving* money moves us away from all kinds of evil, too? It certainly does, and freedom from evil is a beautiful thing.

The dangers of money and wealth often wreak havoc in our personal relationships and professional ambitions. And tragically, the same can happen in our local churches and the overarching Body of Christ itself.

Throughout His life and teachings, Jesus issues definitive warnings for those of us who have accumulated any sort of surplus of financial resources. It is as if He is saying...*Watch out! Treat your money as though you were handling fire or even dynamite. Use it wisely and safely, and harness its energy to do good by disposing of it freely and joyfully.* Properly managed, one "dynamite blast" of generous giving can erode the foundations of poverty in a third-world community. One blast can crack away at the spiritual darkness that many individuals and communities around the world currently face.

Yes, under God's guiding hand, money that is strategically and generously given can do all of those things and more. But, of course, we live in a fallen world...one in which our culture and our money conspire to own us. They constantly whisper (and sometimes scream) that more is better, and they relentlessly attempt to carry us further away from the "true life."

In this week's devotions, we'll learn about some of the hindrances of giving. Fear, worry, greed, loss – these and many more can easily distract us from a pattern of consistent, joyful generosity. Yet it's comforting to know that Jesus tackled such issues head on during His ministry. So this week you will be studying His teachings warning about the pitfalls of your money and your "stuff." And by moving away from these pitfalls, we'll naturally move toward the freedom that comes with the true, generous life.

forward thinking

Generosity helps free us
from the dangers of money.

Excessive worry

"Therefore I tell you, do not worry about your life, what you will eat or drink;
or about your body, what you will wear. Is not life more important than food,
and the body more important than clothes?"
Matthew 6:25

A smoldering fire burns deep within every human being. It's called fear. We may try to camouflage it with our bravado and our boasting, but it is there all the same. Fear of what? Our vulnerability to the harshness of life. Worry is the evidence of our deepest fears.

Jesus speaks to people who are immersed with fear and worry. They worry about death; they worry about where the next meal is coming from. And they worry about having enough stuff to protect them from the elements. We are no different. We have just packed a little bit more insulation into our lives. We are relatively wealthy people. We have thought that our money may buy a few more years, keep us well-fed, and keep us protected from all the bad things that might otherwise happen.

We must not pretend these fears do not exist, that they are not gnawing at our souls. And we must take a hard look at our tendency to address these fears by simply acquiring a bit more stuff.

Jesus' first point: Take a look at the living things of creation. See any worry there? No, what you see is a creation quite at peace with itself because the Heavenly Father feeds it.

Worrying, Jesus points out, never extended life by a single hour. Some of us are going to want to resist this challenge by protesting that we never worry. You will never see us wringing our hands, sitting in a state of panic, paralyzed into inaction because fear has possessed us. No, but what you will see is many of us working harder and harder, keeping our eyes upon the bank account, always aware of who might be catching up to us, mindful of all the indicators that might predict downturns in the market or the value of the things we own. No worry in all of this?

Pagans are great worriers. Why? Because they do not have any sense of a God who cares for them. No God who is intimately aware of their lives and needs. No God who responds to prayer.

But Biblical people are quite aware of a God who is Father to us all. And when a Father of this magnitude is present to us, worry melts like ice in a hot sun. Or it should.

In what ways does wealth create worry? In what ways does wealth relieve worry?

Enslaved heart

Now a man came up to Jesus and asked, "Teacher, what good thing must I do
to get eternal life?" "Why do you ask me about what is good?" Jesus replied.
"There is only one good. If you want to enter life, obey the commandments...."
"All of these I have kept," the young man said. "What do I still lack?"
Jesus answered, "If you want to be perfect, go, sell your possessions and
give to the poor, and you will have treasure in heaven. Then come, follow Me."
When the young man heard this, he went away sad, because he had great wealth.
Matthew 19:16-17, 20-22

The confident young man probably shouldn't have asked what it
was he was lacking. For the Savior hit him with a challenge and an
invitation that no one in his right mind would have put forward. "Go
sell everything you have, give the proceeds to the poor, and come
and follow Me."

Herein lies one of the great Christian enigmas. Does Christ really
want any person to have (much less enjoy) wealth, or not? Why
does Jesus give this confrontational command when others in the
Biblical literature (both Old and New Testaments) appear free to
have many possessions?

The only conceivable answer is this: Jesus, looking into this man's
heart, knew that his wealth owned him. That he defined himself
with his money and his status. Or to use religious language: His
money and his lifestyle was his god, and he worshipped it all.

It was this abnormal attachment that stood between him and the
eternal life he asked Jesus about. Not a lot different from the attachment Abraham apparently felt to his only son, Isaac. In both cases,
men were challenged to lay their "gods" on the altar. One man, his
son; the other, his money.

"When the young man went away, he felt sad because he had great wealth." One wonders, how long did this young man live with that sadness? A few days? Months? A lifetime? A laser beam of conviction had been shot into his soul, and his real god had been exposed.

What if the young man had said to Jesus: "I'll do it. I'll meet you here tomorrow after I've divested myself of everything." Can you imagine Jesus saying, as heaven had answered Abraham many years before, "Stop, now I know that you love me."?

Some think that the young man actually thought this challenge through and did what Jesus asked. I'm doubtful. If only that I suspect Matthew would have told us the end of the story had that happened.

The would-be generous giver must read this story many, many times. Memorizing it would not hurt. It speaks to the chief temptation any successful or wealthy person has: When does all of this become a god to me? And what if Jesus were to put the challenge to me?

Scripture teaches us that we can't serve both God and money. How does wealth tend to capture your heart like the rich young ruler?

Pull of greed

Someone in the crowd said to Him [Jesus], "Teacher, tell my brother to divide the inheritance with me."Jesus replied, "Man, who appointed me a judge or an arbiter between you?" Then He said to them, "Watch out! Be on your guard against all kinds of greed; a man's life does not consist in the abundance of his possessions."

Luke 12:13-15

The crowds were huge that day, the interaction fierce. Teachers like Jesus were used to the give and take that came from those who were closest. There were questions and accusations. Brain went against brain. And there were the requests for adjudication, for the teacher (or rabbi) was honored as the judge in unsettled disputes.

Here is a case in point. Two brothers were obviously locked in a quarrel. There may have been a recent death in the family, as the inheritance was in dispute. The older brother had seized the entire family inheritance for himself, as was his right according to custom. The firstborn possessed everything.

The claimant in this story, a younger brother, demanded a share of the inheritance. But he had no case except to appeal to the grace or generosity of his older brother. And that didn't seem to be going well.

forward thinking

The antidote to materialism is generosity.

In his desperation, the younger brother appealed to Jesus. "Speak to him for me," you can almost hear him saying. "He likes You; he'll listen to You."

But for reasons unexplained, Jesus refused the assignment. Why? It was not in alignment with His mission and priorities. But He does use the episode as a platform for some remarks that ought to go to the center of the heart of a would-be generous giver.

His principle: Watch out for all kinds of greed. In this case, there were two kinds: the greed of the older brother, who clearly intended to keep everything for himself. The younger brother, however, was also greedy: Apparently he was prepared to do anything to grasp a portion of the estate. Both brothers risked relationships – both their own and among other family members – over money.

Greed – the drive to increase one's bank account and to defend it at all costs – is among the most destructive of spiritual forces. It regularly creates conditions of contentiousness, incivility, and alienation. It flows from that darkest part of our beings that believes that we never have enough, that money is the solution to all problems, and that wealth is the key to our personal value as people.

Watch out! Be on your guard! Jesus says, speaking as to a soldier who must be on the highest state of alert. In doing so, Jesus warns us of the true nature of greed: It is a highly destructive force that eats away at the heart. No matter how mature we grow or powerful we become as Christ-followers, we are only a step away from falling into the gravitational pull of greed.

Read the White Elephant story (next page) and answer: Why do you think greed is such a powerful force?

the white elephant of wealth
one couple's journey away from self-focused prosperity

In ancient days, when the king of Siam had an enemy he wanted to torment and destroy, he would send that enemy a very unique gift: a white elephant...a live, albino elephant. These animals were considered sacred in the culture of that day, so the recipient of the elephant had no choice but to intentionally care for the gift. This elephant would take an inordinate amount of the enemy's time, resources, energy, emotions, and finances. Over time, the enemy would destroy himself because of the extremely burdensome process of caring for the white elephant.

Could it be that Satan has made just such a gift to many of us in today's Christian churches? Most every believer in America is rich by the rest of the world's standards, so perhaps our prosperity has come by our acceptance of the "white elephant of wealth"...the self-focused "good life" that consumes most of our energy and has the potential to slowly destroy us.

Jess Correll has battled this white elephant of wealth his whole life. A banking executive and farmer in Kentucky, Jess freely admits that he has always struggled with greed. He and his older brother, Vince, decided at an early age that they wanted to be the "richest men in Kentucky." They bought their first bank when they were in their mid-twenties, which started a long streak of more bank and real estate deals. Jess eventually lost his first marriage because of his obsession with success.

Yet Jess noticed something in Vince that he didn't have...a spirit of selfless generosity. Vince loved to give and share freely with those in need, and this impacted his younger brother tremendously. When Vince died of brain cancer at age 38, Jess made the decision to better follow his brother's godly example.

Soon after, Jess met and married his second wife, Angela, and together they decided that they would always put faith and family ahead of business. Jess still continued to grow his banks...but he did so in a way that his wealth would no longer be his white elephant. He discovered how to give away significant amounts of his private bank stock through a private foundation, and soon his bank's senior management team joined in this giving, as well.

Jess' father taught him that the antidote to greed is giving away money recklessly. Today, Jess and Angela now give away five to eight times what they spend in a year.

Jess and Angela now give away five to eight times what they spend in a given year. He has learned that truly generous giving stems from one's faith...when you give money away, you depend on God to replenish it so that you can be even more generous in the future.

Jess' father once taught him that the antidote to greed is giving away money recklessly. It took Jess and Angela a while in life to fully understand and appreciate this, but once they did, the white elephant of wealth disappeared. And the freedom and joy this Kentucky couple has experienced through giving far surpasses the temporary pleasures of self-gratification.

>>> Watch a video version of this story at
    GenerousChurch.com/generosity

Greater possibility of loss

"But God said to him, 'You fool! This very night your life will be demanded from you. Then who will get what you have prepared for yourself?' This is how it will be with anyone who stores up things for himself but is not rich toward God."

Luke 12:13-21

Generosity says: "What shall I do? I will find effective ways to share my blessings." Greed says: "I have no place to store my good fortune; I will build more barns so that I can keep it all for myself." And that is what this rich man did.

His new business plan is spelled out in detail: Build more and bigger barns. Everything the man owned would be under his control. Then, he concluded, he would find security and happiness.

However, we who are acquainted with the Bible know exactly where this story is going. The man's business plan did not take into account the variable of death. While this man asserted total control over his assets, he had no control over his longevity.

That night God called in his larger account: Your assets can remain in their big barns. But your life is being taken from you. The "rich fool" had failed to consider the consequences of his choices. In his greed, he ended up losing everything.

The more a person is blessed with influence and with material resources, the more one must think with discernment about consequences. What are the implications of the choices I am making with what I have? There are implications connected with every choice. The fool ignores them; the wise and generous giver considers them thoughtfully.

It is from stories such as this one that would-be generous givers learn an important principle: There is accountability in wealth and influence. The greater the resources at our disposal, the greater the possibility of disaster – unless we are humble and submissive before our God and His purposes for us.

How does our culture encourage you to build bigger barns through wealth accumulation? In light of Scripture, is it wise to do so? Why, or why not?

Myth of independence

"Not long after that, the younger son got together all he had, set off
for a distant country and there squandered his wealth in wild living."

Luke 15:13

For reasons unexplained, the father in Jesus' story gives the
younger son what he asks: his "share" of the estate. And what does
the young man do? He takes off! He disappears without a word of
thanks or explanation.

The young man thinks that he is now independent and free to
go where he wishes, spend his money as he wishes, and pursue
whatever life-objectives he wishes. This is what most people call
freedom: no accountability, no constraints. Take what's yours and
"go for it."

And for a few sentences, it does indeed appear as if he's made a
good decision. The front end of "wild living" does seem attractive to
parts of the human soul. At some time or other, most of us wonder
what it might be like to play "outside the box." However, this wild
living soon came to a pitiful and humiliating halt. Hard times came

forward thinking

Generosity leads us to
greater dependence on God.

(in this case, a famine), his funds were exhausted, and, the Bible tells us, "He began to be in need."

What is this story saying to us, as would-be generous givers? No one likes to be in need. And one of the values of money is that it appears to create a certain level of independence. It is a myth of autonomy that says, "I don't need anyone, and no one is going to intrude upon or control my life."

However, just like the prodigal son, sooner or later life shows us in any number of ways that we are not as independent as we thought, and that money alone cannot buy us out of every difficulty.

The young man in this story discovered this lesson the hard way. Living with pigs is no place for a Jew to end up. Might as well call the place hell. Here, in this hell, you're not sure that you eat even as well as the pigs eat.

Study this man well in his moment of total defeat. He is where we all end up apart from the grace of God. He is where more than a few find themselves when they nursed the spirit of arrogance and not humility. He is at the place where the only viable option is the road home.

How is the myth of independence that wealth creates reflected in your life? How can you destroy that myth?

Slow drift from God

"No servant can serve two masters. Either he will hate the one and
love the other, or he will be devoted to the one and despise the other.
You cannot serve both God and money."

Luke 16:13

"No servant can serve two masters." In ancient days, servants and
slaves were a familiar part of the culture. A slave was the possession
of his master. And, similarly, the responsibility of a servant was to
be totally dedicated to the wishes and benefits of the one for whom
he worked. A servant was to be so committed to the interests of
the master, he would hate (or find abhorrent) the notion of serving
anyone else at the same time.

No one seems to have disagreed with the basic premise of Jesus'
assertion. But then, Jesus turned the observation in another direction. The same, He says, is true when it comes to God and money.

Note the power of the polarity here: money and God. In a sense
they are total adversaries. It is virtually impossible for a person to
be totally committed to financial matters and have a hope of any
serious commitment to God. Money is a form of power, and it often
becomes a power that is adverse or alternative to the power and
influence of God.

Many of us will want to deny the force of Jesus' statement. Better
that we capitulate to it. Better that we acknowledge that when we
have a surplus of money, we are always on the cusp of drifting
away from God. With money we have less to pray for. With money,
we have less of a sense of dependence upon Him. With money, we
are tempted toward the myth of self-sufficiency. And with money,
we face the constant stress of aligning our priorities with Kingdom

purposes. Oh, this too: With money we are forever fighting pride and losing humility. Those are the possibilities.

You can't serve both, Jesus tells His crowd of listeners. The implication is unmistakable; make up your mind, and make it up every day. Which do you serve? You can't serve both. It is an intimidating mystery. No wonder it says in verse fourteen that the Pharisees mocked Jesus. What else can one do if he feels threatened by the truth?

In what ways do you find yourself tempted to serve money instead of God?

Increasing vulnerability

"Do not store up for yourselves treasures on earth,
where moth and rust destroy, and where thieves break in and steal."
Matthew 6:19

Most of us are forever collecting things – treasures if you will. Children collect stuffed animals, toys, lucky stones, or special mementos. Teenagers collect music, video games, and clothes. And we adults? Money, expensive playthings, and trophy homes.

And why do we do this? Perhaps it has something to do with the attempt to add to our own personal sense of value. I'm a better person than someone else because I live in a larger home. Or maybe it has to do with our perceived need for security. If I have this much more at my disposal, I'm that more insulated from catastrophe. Then again, having more than I really need may be bound up in the issue of power. The more I have, the more weight I have to throw around.

Storing up treasure...wherever Jesus goes He sees people doing this in one way or another. He is aware of the farmer (the rich fool) who builds bigger barns to store greater volumes of crops. He knows of the Pharisee who works the legal technicalities of religion to deny his parents financial support so that he may have more himself. And He has met the young community leader who is filthy rich and afraid to part with what he has in order to follow Christ. He has seen each of these, and many more, storing up what they have: hiding it, protecting it, expanding it, bragging about it.

"Don't do it!" the Lord cries out. Holding on to everything makes you increasingly vulnerable. Your treasure will be eroded, eaten away by rust and moth. Your precious things will be destroyed. The moth (a living tiny thing) will clean out your expensive wardrobe. And rust (an insidious agent of nature) will weaken whatever you have in your garage or out in the yard. Then there are thieves (human elements) who rub their hands in anticipation of taking away your jewelry, your car, your flat screen TV.

This is not about a responsible savings plan. Nor is it about prudent investments. Rather, it is about a mindset that puts its trust in the accumulation of things and forgets that, in the final analysis, God is our security, our provider, our judge. You know you've fallen into the kind of perspective of which Jesus speaks when all you think about is how can I get more, how can I protect what I've got, how can I make sure that every one knows how much I'm worth? Not a good way to live, our Lord says.

What are some ways that you've stored up treasures on earth? ...in heaven?

week 2 discussion

The following is a summary of the ideas and questions from this week's devotions. Use them for personal reflection or small group discussion, and consider journaling to record your thoughts and impressions.

forward thinking

Which of these "forward thinking" points has the most meaning for you? Least meaning? Why?

Generosity helps free us from the dangers of money.

The antidote to materialism is generosity.

Generosity leads us to greater dependence on God.

impact from the White Elephant story

What was the most important thing you learned from the story of Jess and Angela Correll? Have you personally battled the "white elephant" of wealth? What do you think "giving away money recklessly" really means? How likely are you to do that?

reflection questions

1 In what ways does wealth create worry? In what ways does wealth relieve worry?

2 Scripture teaches us that we can't serve both God and money. How does wealth tend to capture your heart like the rich young ruler?

3 Why do you think greed is such a powerful force?

4 How does our culture encourage you to build bigger barns through wealth accumulation? In light of Scripture, is it wise to do so? Why, or why not?

5 How is the myth of independence that wealth creates reflected in your life? How can you destroy that myth?

6 In what ways do you find yourself tempted to serve money instead of God?

7 What are some ways that you've stored up treasures on earth?...in heaven?

week 3

moving toward
trust

moving toward
trust

"It is more blessed to give than to receive" (Acts 20:35).

In this one simple sentence, Jesus expresses a truth so deep we could spend eternity trying to plumb its depths. Like many of Jesus' sayings, it's a paradox. Our human nature screams out just the opposite: *It is more blessed to receive than to give...accumulation is better than distribution!*

Ultimately, the true life of generosity requires trust on our parts... trust that Jesus' words from Acts 20 are true and that our sacrifices will result in beautiful rewards for us and the recipients of our gifts – sometimes here on earth, and sometimes reserved for us in heaven. In short, generosity comes down to an act of faith in Him who not only first modeled the practice of joyful giving, but also promised the blessings that come alongside.

So far in our devotionals, we've learned that by dwelling on the generous nature of the Trinity and the generous culture of the early church, our hearts and minds can undergo transformation. We've learned about the freedom that generosity brings from the entanglements of wealth. And now its time to reflect on a truth so compelling, that when we really "get it," it takes our breath away: God promises great opportunity to those who give from a pure heart.

Over the next week, we will explore God's unblushing promises of opportunity in response to our generosity – joy, eternal reward, life prosperity, contentment, community, and freedom, to name a few. Yet we must have faith and trust in Him that such promises will come true.

God blesses us with His money for a short time on earth, He empowers us with the Holy Spirit to equip us to give generously, and then He rewards us in so many ways when we trust Him, follow through, and give.

What a tribute to His amazing grace!

forward thinking — Great blessings accompany the generous life.

Overflowing joy

And now, brothers, we want you to know about the grace that God has given
the Macedonian churches. Out of the most severe trial, their overflowing joy
and their extreme poverty welled up in rich generosity.

2 Corinthians 8:1-2

In all the Bible, one would be hard-pressed to find two chapters (2
Corinthians 8 and 9) that speak more beautifully and more bluntly
to the issue of generous giving? Here is Christianity at its best.

The Macedonian church! No sooner had Paul started it up, than the
small, struggling congregation began to prove itself...especially in
the area of generosity. They were steeped in numbing poverty and
suffering. Yet, these congregations also made a decision to "joyfully" give to those struggling hundreds of miles away in Judea.

Paul's description of these remarkable Macedonians deserves our
close attention. Paul holds them up as his model for the consummate generous giver...yet they are among the poorest people we shall
ever know about. In that very fact is a powerful message that must
penetrate our hearts. For our instinct is to associate generous giving
with the efforts of wealthy and powerful people. Yet Paul reserves his
greatest accolades for people on the bottom of the economic ladder.

forward thinking Generous givers experience
a life full of joy.

Note Paul's description of the conditions in which these people gave. They were in "severe trial," which probably alludes to stiff persecution. They were poor in the extreme. Yet neither of these two facts deterred them from asking the question: How much can we give? The phrase "welled up" in some translations provides a vivid word picture. One envisions a spout of water coming up from the ground – generous giving gushing out of lives marked with suffering and scarcity. The amount given is not important; the proportion means everything.

Paul does not stop there. "They urged us (on their own) to share in this service to the saints." Imagine! No fund-raising effort, no high-pressure persuasion, no gimmicks. They simply wanted to do this, in fact pleaded for the privilege.

Paul admits to a sense of surprise about the Macedonian's methods. "They gave themselves first to the Lord and then to us..." Who asked them to do this? Who told them that this was the virtuous way? We're not told. Perhaps the Holy Spirit? No matter. Paul is astonished at their maturity.

In spite of the fact that they were among the most economically deprived people in the New Testament, they were committed to giving. And their giving was marked with "overflowing joy." Consequently, we know that the witness of this community of people exploded across the region. Soon people were talking about this excited band of people who had found new faith. They were poor, had all the normal relational and economic problems churches usually have, and still had a fixation on the coming of Christ. But above all that: We know they were generous givers. Paul says so.

Describe a time when you experienced the joy of generous giving.

An abundant harvest of Kingdom gain

Remember this: Whoever sows sparingly will also reap sparingly,
and whoever sows generously will also reap generously.

2 Corinthians 9:6

Call it Generous Giving 101. First, a simple word picture. An ancient farmer walks down the furrows of his newly plowed field. He reaches into his seed bag for a handful of seed and begins to spread it. Consciously or unconsciously, he makes a decision at that instant: Will he permit the seed to flow abundantly through his fingers into the soil, or will he tighten his fingers so that the seed flows sparingly.

What might influence him to hold back? Fear that he might not have enough seed left at the end of the furrow? Concern that seed is so expensive that he cannot afford to waste even a pinch of it? Doubt in the quality of the soil or the quantity of the coming rain, making him hesitate to invest all of his seed in one spot?

On the other hand, the farmer may know his soil well and be supremely optimistic of a good harvest. Perhaps he is confident of prevailing weather patterns. Most of all, he could be a farmer who has ultimate trust in the God of nature and simply anticipates good things from the hand of his Heavenly Father. In all these cases, the farmer will lavish the soil with his seed.

Paul likens the perspectives of these two kinds of farmers with that of the generous giver. The abundance of our harvest will be in direct proportion to the level of generosity with which we sow our seed. The financial gifts of the generous giver, like seed, initiate a process toward harvest. Great giving invites great harvests. Cautious, reluctant, or grudging giving yields meager harvests.

As in the real world of planting and harvesting, God is the giver of the "increase" as we sow our seeds of generosity. This harvest is made up of changed lives – lives redeemed from evil, lives snatched from poverty, ignorance, disease, oppression. The harvest is in churches, colleges, mission organizations, community development and home building. And what a harvest it is...enjoyed most by those who reached into their "seed-bags" and threw out the seed with a certain reckless generosity.

Remember: The soil is good, the climate is perfect. And the giver of the increase (our Father) is ready to provide the harvest.

What role does faith play in your ability to "sow generously" for an abundant harvest of Kingdom gain?

Eternal reward

"But store up for yourselves treasures in heaven, where moth and
rust do not destroy, and where thieves do not break in and steal.
For where your treasure is there your heart will be also."
Matthew 6:20-21

What does it mean to store treasures in heaven? Obviously one
cannot ship gold, securities, and foreign sports cars there. So
treasures in heaven must mean, first of all, a new kind of currency.

We use dollars in the United States, the peso in some of the Latin
countries, euros (more and more) in Europe, and yen in Japan.
Currencies appropriate to the country. The generous giver wisely
maximizes his investments in the currency of heaven.

Heaven deals with the currency of love, grace, kindness, mercy, and
benevolence. It recognizes the currency of humility, service, and
witness. It honors the currency of defense on behalf of the widow
and the orphan, the weak and the poor, the sick and the aged. These
and all other attitudes and actions in the family of godly behavior
are seen by heaven in the context of currency exchange.

As we grow in our adoption of these convictions and values, the
God of heaven (dare we call Him the Grand "Banker") takes note of
these things and records them to our account. At first it seems an
almost silly perspective, to think of righteous transactions in such
a fashion. But we live this way on earth. Why not, for a moment,
see its heavenly parallel? At least that is the way Jesus appears to
be thinking here.

The good thing about treasures in heaven is that there is no depres-
sion or devaluation there. Our treasures on deposit in heaven are
not susceptible to those original erosive agents: moths, rust, and
thieves and other things like them.

Furthermore, and here Jesus shows that He has our number; He knows that one's heart is always inclined in the direction of the stored-up treasure. That is why so many of us call our brokers, check the Dow Jones Average, and subscribe to newsletters with their economic forecasts. That's where a large part of our attentions are focused, where our "heart" is. But if the real treasure is being stored up in heaven, the heart will follow.

How are you seeking to cultivate an eternal perspective in your life that will impact how you spend and give your treasures?

Life prosperity

You will be made rich in every way so that you can be generous on every occasion, and through us your generosity will result in thanksgiving to God.

2 Corinthians 9:11

Following the plan of cheerful giving comes the promise. It is a promise made by God, who originated the notion of generous giving.

"You will abound in every good work," Paul wrote to the Corinthians. Clearly, Paul had seen this sort of thing happen over and over again. When a person begins to give on the basis of enthusiastic generosity, all sorts of things in life begin to fall into place. Blessings abound, one's effectiveness as a Christian increases, and spiritual maturity deepens into Christ-likeness. Abundance flows from the generous life.

Paul suggested that there is every reason to believe that God will restore to the giver that which was previously given away. Of course, we must be careful not to fall into a "tit-for-tat" mentality; not every gift comes back. However, Paul noticed that generous people often discover all kinds of new wealth (spiritual and material) that permit them to expand the parameters of their generosity. Generous giving is often its own reward as one becomes increasingly excited about giving of self and the spiritual gifts that God has invested in us.

The final result is that thanksgiving will be given to God. One person's gift becomes the cause of a cry of praise from a score of others. What more could a generous giver want than the satisfaction of knowing that one small sacrifice caused a bountiful number of others to lift their hearts to heaven in worship?

But what else happens when a person gives cheerfully and sacrificially? The needs of God's people are met. Resources moved from one place to another can alleviate the suffering and deprivation in other parts of Christ's body. Imagine the changed life and destiny of a child, the healing of someone desperately ill, the rearrangement of life for someone who would not have been able to see, hear, or move. Think of families rejoined, communities rebuilt, churches renewed. Rejoice in the notion of people encountering the love of Jesus Christ for the first time and discovering the power to break addictions, patterns of sin, and ways of destructive life. Yes, the needs of God's people are met.

A concert of thanksgiving rises toward heaven. People rise from their lethargy and begin to exalt the name of God, for they have felt His love through the actions of His people.

The genuineness of Christian witness is underscored. "Men will praise God for the obedience that accompanies your confession..." To put it another way, the world has discovered that the religion of the generous giver is not a religion of words but of loving action.

Those whose lives have been touched will lift up prayers of praise and thanksgiving for the generous giver. The loop of blessing is completed in such a fashion. Love given abounds in love returned, and the body of Christ revels in its circle of giving and thanksgiving.

This lovely symphony in praise of generous giving is Paul's benediction upon the man or woman who finds it a joy to to be gracious. In contrast to all the selfishness so easily found in our world, this is a refreshing contrast – a testimony to everything Jesus died for and meant to establish when He called a company of generous givers to follow Him.

Read the Real Prosperity story (next page) and answer: What does life prosperity mean to you? How does generosity contribute to this?

the real prosperity of generosity
one couple's journey of giving it all to God

Give, and God will give back to you financially...that's the basic message of what's commonly called the "prosperity gospel," a teaching that has pervaded many American churches today.

But is it true?

Someone once said, "Any gospel that is true in America but not in Africa is no gospel at all." Think about this for a moment. If you were born in a third-world culture in Africa or India, for example, odds are you would grow up in a household of poverty. But if you became a Christian in that situation, God probably wouldn't instantly bless you with financial prosperity...even if you were generous with your resources. In fact, you might live your entire life as a follower of Jesus Christ struggling to simply survive.

The reason the prosperity gospel appeals to so many in America is that it is based on a half-truth. Though God does want to make us "rich in every way" (2 Corinthians 9:10-11), the prosperity gospel aims too low by focusing solely on the financial blessings God *sometimes* provides when we give generously. God doesn't guarantee financial prosperity when we are generous, but He does promise life prosperity to the generous giver – such as gaining wisdom, joy, peace, friendships, future eternal reward, and so on.

The life of Stanley Tam is a powerful testimony to life prosperity gained when one surrenders his life to God completely. In the mid-1950s, Stanley gave up control of his struggling business to God by placing 51% of the stock in a private foundation. If God chose to prosper the business, Stanley would use 51% of the profits to

spread the Gospel around the
world. At the time Stanley did
this, he was making only $14
per week!

Slowly the business began
to turn around. And over the
years, Stanley realized that
perhaps 51% wasn't enough;
perhaps God wanted it all.
So eventually he and his wife
Juanita made the decision to put
100% of the stock in the foundation.
They chose to draw a relatively moderate
salary from the business and give all of the profits away.

Stanley gave up control of his struggling business to God, and since the 1950s, more than $115 million in profits have been given away to Kingdom work.

The result of their decision? Over the past half-century, the company has generated over $115 million in profits that have been given away to Kingdom work! And if you have the pleasure of meeting Stanley Tam today (in his 90s), you will find a contented man who has lived a life of purpose – to be used as a tool in God's hand to make money for Kingdom work.

Surely Stanley has been made rich in every way and lived a life of real prosperity.

>>> **Watch a video version of this story at
GenerousChurch.com/generosity**

Real community

All believers were together and had everything in common. Selling their possessions and goods, they gave to anyone as he had need. Every day they continued to meet together in the temple courts. They broke bread in their homes and ate together with glad and sincere hearts, praising God and enjoying the favor of all the people. And the Lord added to their number daily those who were being saved.

Acts 2:44-47

We have three descriptions of the financial activities of the early church. The first of the three blends in with the opening description of their new life together as followers of Christ. "Selling their possessions and goods, they gave to anyone as he had need" (Acts 2:45). It is a noteworthy commentary on the primary expression of faith in the lives of these people.

We struggle to know exactly what this simple sentence means. Was this a spontaneous explosion of generosity? Had it been taught? Did it continue for a long time, or was it an immediate and temporary expression?

The previous sentence describes an intensity of community: "All the believers were together." And it goes on to say, "(they) had

forward thinking

God's power abounds in a community of generous givers.

everything in common." In other words there was no separateness between the Christ-followers. The rich and the poor came together, and there was an overflow of sharing, so much so that it seemed as if the fellowship engaged in share-and-share-alike.

Down through the centuries, there have been Christians who have taken this account so seriously that they have espoused a communal way of life in which there was no private ownership. Others have suggested that this passage provides merely a temporary description of Christian life together, one that did not last for very long.

Perhaps, it would be more helpful and more useful if we went to the deeper principle here: Profound conversion of heart produces a natural generosity. The power of Christ unbound the selfish heart. It generated a love and compassion between people that was so intense that no one could hold on to anything extra when someone else appeared in personal need.

That alone is sufficient to take away from this text. What's to learn? We cannot say that we are people of faith and remain stingy, greedy, and unfeeling toward human need. We cannot say we belong to the Christian movement if there is not a delight in sharing resources that will lift another out of hardship and into brightness of opportunity and abundant life.

This much we know about that first church: It abounded with generous givers.

Describe a time when generosity produced great unity in your church, small group, workplace, family, or circle of friends.

Freedom from arrogance

Command those who are rich in this present world not to be arrogant nor to
put their hope in wealth, which is so uncertain, but to put their hope in God, who
richly provides us with everything for our enjoyment. Command them to do good,
to be rich in good deeds, and to be generous and willing to share. In this way they
will lay up treasure for themselves as a firm foundation for the coming age,
so that they may take hold of the life that is truly life.

1 Timothy 6:17-19

Every privilege and blessing has accompanying temptations. People
of wisdom understand this, and do all they can to ensure that the
temptations are quickly spotted and defeated when they present
themselves.

It appears to be Paul's observation that two of the more common
temptations for people who have been materially blessed are an
attitude of arrogance and a tendency to believe that wealth can
solve all problems.

Arrogance and pride: They are postures of personality that infer
(consciously or unconsciously) that one knows more, can do more,
and is worth more than anyone else. The arrogance of the wealthy
leads to the belief that one can live above the rules and buy oneself
into anything or out of anything. In Proverbs 8.13, wisdom is heard
to say, "I hate pride and arrogance..."

The temptation to "put (one's) hope in wealth" is the second temptation. In this time of prosperity in which we live, it is not difficult
to see why a young man or woman would think that there is no
problem which cannot be solved by cash.

Nebuchadnezzar looked out upon Babylon and succumbed to both
temptations when he said, "Is not this the great Babylon I have built

as the royal residence, by my mighty power and for the glory of my majesty?"

"The words were still on his lips," Scripture says, when a voice came from heaven pronouncing judgment upon him. The man spent seven years separated from it all.

How do we counter the temptations of arrogance and pride associated with material goods? Paul gives us the answer in this passage. When we do good, when we are rich in good deeds, when we are generous and willing to share, then we take hold of the life that is truly life. Instead of letting money be a destructive force in our lives that creates havoc, we harness the power of money to help others, to make a difference in the Kingdom, and in the process we find true life.

Why do you think pride often accompanies wealth? How do you think generosity helps free you from this arrogance?

Demonstration of real faith

This is how we know what love is: Jesus Christ laid down his life for us.
And we ought to lay down our lives for our brothers. If anyone has
material possessions and sees his brother in need but has no pity on him,
how can the love of God be in him? Dear children, let us not love with
words or tongue but with actions and in truth.
1 John 3:16-18

The Gospel came into an essentially loveless world. Cruelty, vengeance, oppression and slavery were the order of the day. A small band of people expanded out into the world, spreading the word of a new way of looking at reality. Its core conviction was love.

But what is love? Certainly it is not the sentimental, romantic, feelings-driven thing we hear about in songs and on greeting cards. Nothing tough or world-changing about that kind of love.

In this passage, John explains love and what difference it makes. What is love? "Jesus Christ laid down His love for us. And we ought to lay down our lives for our brothers." That's it in a nutshell. We are loved, and we are called to love!

The love that established Christianity was a total commitment. It demanded not only one's possessions, one's reputation, but one's life. Anything short of that was not love. Once that is established and one has declared him- or herself willing to die for a spouse, for children, for friends, everything else comes easy. And John knows this.

And that is why he backs off a bit to something a bit more "daily": If anyone sees a brother in need and has the resources to meet that need and feels no pity and does nothing about the situation, the love of God is not in him. Simple as that!

This is generous giving language. It's generous giving thinking. The genuineness of faith is demonstrated when one learns to discern need, feel authentic pity or compassion, and then chooses to bring resources to the point of need. Yes, that's generous giving.

No wonder John summarizes thusly: "Let us not love in words or tongue (which is what we are often tempted to do) but with actions and truth." Can it be said any better?

Come to think of it, John saw this kind of love on an almost daily basis in the life of his mentor, Jesus. Slowly this kind of thinking claimed his soul, and now he was out to convince others to live and think the same way. And it worked!

Name an example from your life in which you gave to someone, financially or otherwise, out of a deep, compassionate sense of love.

week 3 discussion

The following is a summary of the ideas and questions from this week's devotions. Use them for personal reflection or small group discussion, and consider journaling to record your thoughts and impressions.

forward thinking

Which of these "forward thinking" points has the most meaning for you? Least meaning? Why?

Great blessings accompany the generous life.

Generous givers experience a life full of joy.

God's power abounds in a community of generous givers.

impact from the Life Prosperity story

What was the most important thing you learned from the story of Stanley and Juanita Tam? What temporal, earthly treasures and opportunities do you suppose they gave up in favor of eternal reward? On a scale of 1 (low) to 10 (high), how likely are you to make such a bold agreement with God about giving generosity?

reflection questions

1   Describe a time when you experienced the joy of giving.

2   What role does faith play in your ability to "sow generously" for an abundant harvest of Kingdom gain?

3   How are you seeking to cultivate an eternal perspective in your life that will impact how you spend and give your treasures?

4   What does life prosperity mean to you? How does generosity contribute to this?

5   Describe a time when generosity produced great unity in your church, small group, workplace, family, or circle of friends.

6   Why do you think pride often accompanies wealth? How do you think generosity helps free you from this arrogance?

7   Name an example from your life in which you gave to someone, financially or otherwise, out of a deep, compassionate sense of love.

moving toward
life

moving toward
life

Everyone can "excel in the grace of giving" (2 Corinthians 8:7).

But how often do we recognize and celebrate those who do? We read the books of excellent Christian writers, we download and listen to sermons from excellent Christian preachers, we know the names of the excellent leaders and visionaries from today's Christian parachurch organizations, and we worship God alongside the music of excellent Christian musicians.

But who is known for their excellence in giving? Which famous figures come to mind? Which everyday people from within your own church walls and in your sphere of influence can truly be called excellent in their giving?

If we look for such people with intentionality, odds are we'll find them. Some people have the Spiritual Gift of giving, and the trail of their natural generosity is not hard to track. Others may have found it difficult to develop consistent patterns of giving, but they persevered and now set a wonderful example of the generous life.

Often the stories of great giving do not come from people of extraordinary wealth. True, there are philanthropists who have distributed vast sums of money to people and institutions worthy of their gift. But great giving is not determined by dollar amounts but by the amount of sacrifice. And once that standard is used, the playing field becomes level between the rich and the poor. In other words, one does not have to be rich to be a generous giver.

Over the coming week, we'll discover how everyone can excel in the grace of giving as we look at seven principles that can ignite a lifetime of generosity. We'll begin by making sure our hearts are framed with proper motives, next we'll focus on the importance of incorporating love into our giving, and then we'll explore the disciplines of secrecy, focus, and planning...all with the goal of finishing well when it comes to our giving.

And this pursuit will help lead us to the life that is truly life – true life for us, and true life for those that are blessed by our generosity.

forward thinking

Everyone can excel in the grace of giving.

Examine your heart first, give second

"Therefore, if you are offering your gift at the altar and there remember that
your brother has something against you, leave your gift there in front of the altar.
First go and be reconciled to your brother, then come and offer your gift."

Matthew 5:23

You would think that when someone brings a gift to the temple
that those receiving it would be happy to get it under any circumstances. We assume, under the best of circumstances, that the gift
would relieve the oppression of the poor, underwrite the expenses
of the temple, or contribute to the income of the clergy. Perhaps it
might even open the door for some new "program" or expansion of
temple property.

But here is Jesus putting a condition on gifts. Here is Christ, in
effect, saying that giving must be preceded by certain actions that
are inherently spiritual and relational. In fact, He appears to be
discouraging giving if one has not given careful attention to other
issues...such as the quality of relationship between the would-be
giver and his or her "brother."

You have approached the altar with your gift, He says, and sud-
denly you are caused to remember that there is a broken relationship out there....with your "brother." In this case the "brother" may
be a relative, a friend, a working colleague. You've offended him;
there is a significant breach in your relationship. Before you can
give, you must repair the relational damage. Jesus' remedy: Leave
the gift in front of the altar, find your "brother," reconcile, and then
come back and complete the "transaction."

There's something to think about here. Namely, that Jesus regards
giving as a whole-person event. The gift on the altar is not impres-
sive to Him if it is not preceded by a "gift" of another kind in another
part of life. In this case: the gift of reconciliation whether it means

asking forgiveness or giving it. Leave your gift where it is and go to your "brother."

The temptation, of course, for the generous giver is to think that a major gift covers a lot of small issues in another part of one's life. And that might have been true for the religious leaders of those days and, perhaps, even of today. A large gift can close a lot of eyes. But not the eyes of the Lord. God apparently would rather have the giver stay at home with his gift, if he is planning to approach the alter while there is resentment and hostility in the background.

The spiritual life of the generous giver comes more and more into play in these passages. God seeks generous givers. But, first, He seeks generous givers whose hearts are right with Him and with others.

Why do you think Jesus calls us to place relationships above giving?

Give in love

If I give all I possess to the poor and surrender my body to the flames,
but have not love, I gain nothing.

1 Corinthians 13:3

One has to wonder what prompted St. Paul to make such a dramatic statement. Could he have known a few men and women of influence and means who were given to ostentatious demonstrations of generosity, done in such a way that all the blessing that normally comes with giving was denied?

If I give all that I have, even my body...these are extreme gifts. Seemingly the greatest gifts one might offer. But then comes the qualification: Such gifts given without love mean nothing.

Perhaps Paul was thinking of Jesus, who gave His body out of love (Romans 5:8). This is one of the unique dimensions to the Christian view of giving: It must be done out of love. Not because it affects one's tax bracket. Or because it creates notoriety. Or in order to get something in return.

forward thinking Giving accomplishes great things when done in love.

If we were to approach Paul and ask him what he had in mind when he spoke of giving in love, what answers might he offer to our questions? Perhaps he would say that the giver must engage with those to whom he or she gives. There must be a sense of connection.

There must also be a realization of equality. In the eyes of God, the giver is no better than the beneficiary. When love overarches the giving transaction, the sense of brotherhood leaves no room for snobbery. When love enters the picture, there is a mysterious reciprocity between the giver and the receiver. For the giver always finds that something of value is passed back, and it is usually something which money cannot buy.

"If I give...but have no love, I gain nothing." There are those who would rather give money than love. For it may be, in the long run, that the love is more difficult to give than the money itself.

Read the Franklin story (next page) and answer: How has giving to someone else deepened your relationship with that person?

the miracle in Franklin
two couple's journeys, intertwined in an unlikely way

It was a cold day...the kind you don't really want to have a long conversation outside with someone, especially with someone you don't really know. But that's exactly what happened to twenty-somethings Lance and his wife Amy outside a restaurant in their town of Franklin, Tennessee. The two had just finished lunch and were walking to the car when they recognized an older couple they had seen before at their church. They all stopped briefly and started talking.

The issue of money came up as they chatted about a new financial small group class at their church. Soon, Lance acknowledged that he and Amy had paid off $60,000 in debt but still had $10,000 left to go. The older couple asked them what they would do when they were debt free. At first, Amy laughed about the trampoline they had promised their young kids, but then she confided that their real dream was to adopt another child. However, they were committed to be debt free before they did so. Then, quickly, the conversation shifted to lighter things, and before everyone knew it, it was over. Both couples went on their way.

The next day, Lance got an email at work from the older couple, asking if they could come by his house to talk about something important. Lance was skeptical; *perhaps this is going to be some sort of pyramid marketing scheme,* he thought. Still, he agreed to their request. After work, they all met at Lance and Amy's house and went through the obligatory small talk. But then, the unknown couple dropped a bomb: they wanted to pay off Lance and Amy's $10,000 debt so that the young couple could adopt immediately. "How do you spell your name?" the older woman asked, as she got out her checkbook and began writing.

Lance thought, *Are you kidding me? Are you for real? Who does that? Who writes a check for $10,000 to somebody they don't even know?*

Smiling, the couple told Lance and Amy, "Just don't tell anybody it was us and don't act weird toward us at church." And then they drove off. Lance and Amy stood there for ten minutes in total shock. Then they cried and screamed and ran all over the yard and house. It was unbelievable. It was beyond belief.

Lance and Amy were stunned. How amazing and unbelievable that a couple they barely knew would give them $10,000 to achieve their dream of adoption.

Nine months later, when they brought their new adopted daughter Mayla home, they realized that the check the couple had given them was dated exactly nine months prior to Mayla's due date. The $10,000 gift was made right at the time their daughter was conceived. As Lance recalled, it was like God was saying, "I have a baby out there for you right now. I'm not waiting around another two years for you to pay off that debt."

Lance and Amy decided that their encounter with the other couple outside that downtown restaurant wasn't random at all. God had orchestrated everything, weaving their callings and journies together to write a beautiful story for His Glory.

>>> **Watch a video version of this story at**
   GenerousChurch.com/generosity

Pursue secrecy in giving

"Be careful not to do your 'acts of righteousness' before men, to be seen by them. If you do, you will have no reward from your Father in heaven. So when you give to the needy, do not announce it with trumpets, as the hypocrites do in the synagogues and on the streets, to be honored by men. I tell you the truth, they have received their reward in full. But when you give to the needy, do not let your left hand know what your right hand is doing, so that your giving may be in secret. Then your Father, who sees what is done in secret, will reward you."

Matthew 6:1-4

One of the seldom-mentioned of the traditional spiritual disciplines is that of secrecy. Secrecy involves resisting the temptation to tell others what we have experienced on the spiritual journey. It means refraining from informing others of actions and activities that inflate their view of us. In short, the discipline of secrecy suggests that not everyone needs to know what God is saying to us or what we are doing in response to Him. If it is necessary for others to know, let them find out for themselves.

Many of us were born into a faith tradition that seems bent on telling others everything we have experienced or that we have done as soon as possible. At its best, we call this testifying; at its worst we call it boasting.

Jesus said these words in a time when the rich and famous broadcast their good deeds as "acts of righteousness" whenever possible. They wanted to keep score; they wanted everyone to know just how "good" they were. This of course led to a kind of competition and, from there, to a self-justification. "Look everyone! See how righteous I am."

Our Lord despises this mentality and opts for its absolute opposite: secrecy. Make your righteousness known to everyone else, He says, and the blessing that might have come from heaven will disappear.

If you desire applause for everything you do, then applause you'll probably get. And applause will be the sum total of your giving. But don't expect heaven to join in.

Jesus has just unfolded for us one of the prime elements in the concept of generous giving. Generous givers lean in the direction of secrecy when they engage in "acts of righteousness." Their spiritual maturity makes them immune from the need to be praised by others. It causes them to anticipate God's approval and to settle for that.

Sometimes such secrecy is impossible. Better, however, to embrace this discipline, to make the attempt to act in quietness than to bend to the temptation of the opposite.

How should we balance the call to secrecy with the importance of sharing our giving stories?

Giving to the church

[The Lord said to Moses,]
"With his own hands he is to bring the offering made to the Lord by fire."
Leviticus 7:30

Leviticus is hardly the book most people would want to read for a spiritual jumpstart on a new day. It is filled with long, detailed descriptions of various laws and rituals, which Moses taught to the Israelites during their sojourn in the desert. Yet by reading it, we learn something about the themes that were important to the first generations of people headed to the promised land, which in turn set in motion a new way of life and conviction for the people of God.

The first several chapters, a certain phrase appears again and again that will interest the generous giver: "Bring an offering." These chapters detail many of the ways people were asked to give to the Lord, along with a description of how that offering should be presented, what it meant, and what the priest would do with it.

Leviticus 7:28 describes the fellowship offering – an expression of thanksgiving or gratitude – to be brought to the tabernacle "with (one's) own hand." In other words, it is not something to be delegated or done impersonally. Someone who wanted to acknowledge that he has been blessed with abundance expressed his thanks by carrying his offering himself to the priest. Through it, the Israelites were reminded of a deeply personal element to their expression of faith and generosity.

Part of this offering was to go to the priests, who were charged with maintaining the spiritual life of the community (Leviticus 7:31, 35-36). The message? At the core of the spiritual life of any group of people, there must be some organization and some appointed people to keep it going. Giving to the Lord and to His purposes means giving toward this "spiritual overhead."

What is most interesting about the detailed instructions that dominate Leviticus is how seriously the act of generous giving is taken in their corporate spiritual life. As the architecture of their walk with God is developed, giving and the way it is to be done are at the center of faith.

What is your attitude toward giving to your local church? Do you appreciate and enjoy it, or is it a chore? Why?

Give every day in light of *that* day

"That servant who knows his master's will and does not get ready or does not do what his master wants will be beaten with many blows. But the one who does not know and does things deserving punishment will be beaten with few blows. From everyone who has been given much, much will be demanded; and from the one who has been entrusted with much, much more will be asked."

Luke 12:47-48

Call it a management case study. It is a story told by our Lord that is tied to His concern for personal preparedness.

Jesus had been speaking about future times. His language was startling and a bit disconcerting. About one thing there can be no confusion: A time is coming when history will be interrupted, a time when God is going to bring the earth and its peoples to judgment. The Bible is very plain about this. Will I, will you, will anyone be ready? The Savior's point is equally clear: If you want to be ready, live every day as if it is *that* day.

That puts the case study into perspective. If you are a manager, Jesus says, you don't want to run your business in such a way that you will be humiliated should the owner of the business walk through the doors in a surprise visit.

A wise manager takes care of his people and the resources they employ so that the organization is operating smoothly and productively. A foolish manager banks on the fact that the owner won't be around for a while; he abuses His authority, simply assuming that the day of accounting is too far off to worry about.

Don't bet on it, is the Lord's comment.

Would-be generous givers take this story seriously, and order their lives and assets with the biggest possible picture in mind. Not knowing precisely the moment that Jesus will return, the person of means and influence brings everything in life under this discipline: I want to be instantly ready to open the books of my life and my possessions and place them under the scrutiny of God without fear of embarrassment.

What changes do you need to make in your finances in order to prepare yourself for *that* day?

Establish a giving plan

Each man should give what he has decided in his heart to give, not reluctantly
or under compulsion, for God loves a cheerful giver.

2 Corinthians 9:7

In this simple sentence, Paul introduced the idea of a giving plan. We give by commitment and intention, Paul is suggesting. A strategy of giving has been formed in the mind and heart of a Christ-follower.

Although Paul probably wasn't thinking in explicit detail, here are the implications.... A giving plan begins with the settled conviction that what I have earned or what has been given to me is not mine, but God's; I do not have a right to spend it all upon myself or my own interests.

Having said that, what percentage of the possessions God has entrusted to us does He expect us to give away? The Bible's starting point is the tithe.

For some, there may be times when even ten percent seems impossible. For example, we might be deeply in debt or over-committed in

forward thinking

Excellent planning leads to
excellence in giving.

our financial obligations. The important thing, then, is to at least pick a percentage that is small enough to be reachable, yet large enough to stretch one's faith a bit. And yet our goal remains the same: always to be working toward the day when our giving exceeds the simple tithe.

Once we have determined the amount we intend to give, we need to set our priorities in giving. Where shall my gifts go? Some believe that one's primary gift should go to his or her spiritual community: the church. This seems a prudent idea since it is one's community that provides mutual support and challenge for the spiritual journey.

Beyond that priority, each generous giver must listen to the voice of God, and look diligently for opportunities. What organizations of service align with one's sense of call? Some of us will feel compelled to help educate others; others will be drawn to missionary service. Still others will feel compelled to reach out to prisoners or to the homeless. Some are called to help stem the tide of disease, of illiteracy, of poverty. Bear in mind that those who live by Biblical principles are also called to support those institutions that add value to our community as a whole; the arts and service agencies also deserve our support. What is God saying to you?

This is the beginning of a giving plan. These are the kinds of things that a person schemes out in his heart and mind. And according to that plan, he or she gives "cheerfully," and not under duress. This is the kind of giving that God loves – and blesses.

What steps do you need to take to establish a giving plan?

Finish your giving

And here is my advice about what is best for you in this matter: Last year
you were not only the first to give but also to have the desire to do so.
Now finish the work, so that your eager willingness to do it may be
matched by your completion of it, according to your means.

2 Corinthians 8:11

Beware of a religion that moves on the wheels of good intentions.
That's what was going on in Corinth among the Christians. They
were good at saying the right things, even starting right things. But
were they finishers? Not when it came to generous giving.

"You were the first to give," Paul says. "(In fact) you were the first
to have the desire to do so." But that was last year. The problem:
They hadn't followed through. One quite imagines that last year,
the Corinthians had been full of good intentions. There was probably a high level of passion and expressed concern. You can almost
hear them: "We've got to do something!" And everyone agreed.

A year later, their enthusiasm waned considerably, and the Corinthians
need some prodding. Paul commends their "willingness," and yet also
asks in so many words, what is willingness without performance?

Paul was not asking the Corinthians to give everything away in order
to make someone else the more benefited. No, he simply wanted to
see some sort of equilibrium among believers. He wanted those who
were on top to raise others up.

The apostle's thoughtful lines call the would-be generous giver to
think through his intentions and promises. Paul is rather pointed:
It's not enough to talk about giving; we must actually do it.

Finish the work, Corinth. And to all would-be generous givers of that time and today: Finish the work God has given you. Not to do so is to break vows made to God, and not to do so is to leave others to struggle needlessly.

What obstacles in your life stand in the way of the giving God is calling you to do? What is the next thing you can do to overcome these obstacles?

week 4 discussion

The following is a summary of the ideas and questions from this week's devotions. Use them for personal reflection or small group discussion, and consider journaling to record your thoughts and impressions.

forward thinking

Which of these "forward thinking" points has the most meaning for you? Least meaning? Why?

Everyone can excel in the grace of giving.

Giving accomplishes great things when done in love.

Excellent planning leads to excellence in giving.

impact from the Miracle in Franklin story

What was the most important thing you learned from the Miracle in Franklin story? What feelings and emotions do you believe the generous couple experienced by making their gift? What were some lessons about God and joyful generosity that Lance and Amy learned?

reflection questions

1 Why do you think Jesus calls us to place relationships above giving?

2 How has giving to someone else deepened your relationship with that person?

3 How should we balance the call to secrecy with the importance of sharing our giving stories?

4 What is your attitude toward giving to your local church? Do you appreciate and enjoy it, or is it a chore? Why?

5 What changes do you need to make in your finances in order to prepare yourself for *that* day?

6 What steps do you need to take to establish a giving plan?

7 What obstacles in your life stand in the way of the giving God is calling you to do? What is the next thing you can do to overcome these obstacles?

summary of
forward thinking

1   God is the first and most generous giver.
"For God so loved the world that He gave His one and only Son, that whoever believes in Him shall not perish but have eternal life." John 3:16

2   We are most like God when we give.
"Your attitude should be the same as that of Christ Jesus: Who, being in very nature God, did not consider equality with God something to be grasped, but made Himself nothing, taking the very nature of a servant." Philippians 2:5-7

3   When we give, the world takes notice.
"All the believers were one in heart and mind. No one claimed that any of His possessions was his own, but they shared everything they had.... There were no needy persons among them." Acts 4:32-34

4   Generosity helps free us from the dangers of money.
"Therefore I tell you, do not worry about your life, what you will eat or drink; or about your body, what you will wear. Is not life more important than food, and the body more important than clothes?" Matthew 6:25

5   The antidote to materialism is generosity.
"Then He [Jesus] said to them, 'Watch out! Be on your guard against all kinds of greed; a man's life does not consist in the abundance of his possessions.'" Luke 12:15

6   Generosity leads us to greater dependence on God.
"No servant can serve two masters. Either he will hate the one and love the other, or he will be devoted to the one and despise the other. You cannot serve both God and money." Luke 16:13

7   Great blessings accompany the generous life.
"It is more blessed to give than to receive." (Acts 20:35)

8   Generous givers experience a life full of joy.
"We want you to know about the grace that God has given the Macedonian churches. Out of the most severe trial, their overflowing joy and their extreme poverty welled up in rich generosity." 2 Corinthians 8:1-2

9   God's power abounds in a community of generous givers.
"All believers were together and had everything in common. Selling their possessions and goods, they gave to anyone as he had need.... And the Lord added to their number daily those who were being saved."
Acts 2:44-47

10   Everyone can excel in the grace of giving.
"But just as you excel in everything – in faith, in speech, in knowledge, in complete earnestness and in your love for us – see that you also excel in this grace of giving." 2 Corinthians 8:7

11   Giving accomplishes great things when done in love.
"If I give all I possess to the poor and surrender my body to the flames, but have not love, I gain nothing." 1 Corinthians 13:3

12   Excellent planning leads to excellence in giving.
"Each man should give what he has decided in his heart to give, not reluctantly or under compulsion, for God loves a cheerful giver."
2 Corinthians 9:7

moving toward
action
ideas for taking the next step in your giving journey

Now is the time for growth in your generosity. Now is the time for you to keep pushing on, moving forward, moving toward true life... the joyful, generous life that God is calling all of us to live.

So how do we move? Reread pages 86 & 87 and dwell on these three principles from that day's devotional:

1 **Gain Perspective** – Acknowledge that God owns everything. He is the ultimate owner of all we possess, and we are merely stewards of those resources here on Earth to further His glory.

2 **Commit to a Percentage** – Make a firm decision to start today giving a percentage of your income that is small enough to be reachable but big enough to stretch you. Then, commit to grow that percentage each year.

3 **Identify Priorities** – Brainstorm and document a plan of action for your giving. Decide where God is calling you to give (to your church, to the poor, for evangelism, etc.), and outline your plan for how you will make that happen.

action step: complete the giving agreement
(opposite page)

giving agreement

your written declaration that you will continue
moving toward the generous life that is truly life

I, _____, on this ___ day
$\quad$ full name(s) $\quad\quad\quad\quad\quad\quad\quad\quad$ day

of _____, _____ pledge:
$\quad$ month $\quad\quad\quad\quad$ year

☐ **YES,** I acknowledge that God is the ultimate
check $\quad$ owner of everything that I posess, and I am just a
steward of those resources to further His glory.

____ **I COMMIT** immediately to start giving this
enter % $\quad$ percentage of my income to the Lord's work, and
to strive to increase this percentage over time.

☐ **YES,** within one week, I will make a written plan
check $\quad$ of action for my giving, describing where God is
calling me to give and how I will make that happen.

_____
signature

_____
spouse's signature (if applicable)

_____
today's date

about the
authors

Gordon MacDonald – Best-selling author, speaker, pastor, and teacher, Gordon MacDonald has authored numerous books, including *A Resilient Life, Who Stole My Church,* and *Ordering Your Private World,* which won the prestigious Gold Medallion Award. Gordon speaks at numerous conferences for church and business leaders and is presently Interim President of Denver Seminary. He is also an Editor-at-Large for *Leadership Journal.* The MacDonalds live in Canterbury, New Hampshire.

Patrick Johnson – As Vice President of Church Services with The National Christian Foundation, Patrick Johnson works with church leaders in raising the overall tide of generosity and serving givers. He and his wife, Jennifer, have been married for 18 years and have four children.

about
NCF and Affiliates

Since 1982, The National Christian Foundation and our nationwide network of Local Christian Foundation Affiliates has granted more than $2 billion to over 15,000 churches and ministries by serving the charitable giving needs of individuals, families, churches, ministries, and professional advisors. To learn more or to connect with an Affiliate near you, visit:

NationalChristian.com or call **800.681.6223**

share
generosity
with your church

Are you a pastor or ministry leader looking to raise the tide of generosity in your church or ministry and lead your people to greater spiritual maturity through giving?

Are you a lay leader interested in spreading the message of Biblical generosity and stewardship in your church?

If so, sharing this book with your whole congregation or organization is a wonderful way to get started. Churches across the country, for example, are ordering copies of *Generosity* to give or sell to their members, in concert with a four-week sermon series and small-group discussions that match the book's outline. One pastor commented on the growth of generosity in his church…

> "Our church planned a four-week stewardship thrust in the middle of the economic downturn. I wanted something that our people could read, something succinct, Biblical, and motivational. *Generosity* fit the bill! Several hundred of our folks read it, and I'm convinced it has helped us stay close to budget during very trying economic times."

order today at
GenerousChurch.com

Customized, private-labeled versions and discounts on large orders are available.